There IS Happiness
After Incest and
Child Sexual Abuse

Happiness Is Yours!

Claim It !!!

There IS Happiness After Incest and Child Sexual Abuse

CeCe Norwood

Rev. date: 06/12/2019

To order additional copies of this book, contact:
Xlibris
1-888-795-4274
www.Xlibris.com
Orders@Xlibris.com
578908

CONTENTS

DEDICATION

This book is dedicated to my mother, K. LaVerne Redden, who taught me everything I needed to know to be a successful African American Women. I love you Mom.

And To

My precious daughter, Shai Ayn, who has been the greatest person God has brought into my life. Shai, you taught me to not take life so seriously and you continue to shower me with unconditional love. I love you.

And To

All of the beautiful women and men who took the risk to share with me your stories, your pains, and your joys. Your truths have been shared with other survivors as all of our experiences are healing. Your stories and experiences helped crystallized the content of this book, which will spread healing around the world. All of you have contributed to my personal journey to happiness. Thank You.

Acknowledgments

A project of this magnitude cannot be done alone. I sincerely acknowledge and thank Love Ali, Dr. Sharon Barnes, Carolyn Wilson and James F. Loomis who took their precious time to read my manuscript and offer guiding suggestions and wonderful contributions to the finished product. I could not have gotten this project finished without your help.

I was looking long and hard for the book cover that expressed my belief that happiness, following being sexually abused as a child, is possible for all women, when I received a proposal from Kate Hillson. Kate, you got it exactly right. Thank you.

INTRODUCTION

"There *IS* Happiness After Incest and Child Sexual Abuse." This statement is my message to all survivors I meet. For most people who read this statement, however, I know there is immediate doubt. There is immediately doubt, because too often virtually every book you pick up regarding surviving incest and child sexual abuse does not directly address this particular issue. And when you consider the survivors I have spoken to who have been in individual therapy for years, the number of nonbelievers is even greater, I'm sure. But yet this is the question that every incest and child sexual abuse survivor asks in one way or another. Usually the direct question is, "Will this pain ever go away?" The unspoken question is: "Will I every be happy?"

This book is about YOU having an opportunity to find the happiness you deserve in your life because it IS possible to be happy following being a victim of incest and child sexual abuse! I know what I am saying firsthand because I am writing this book as a black woman who was sexually abused by my stepfather, a teenage female cousin, and a friend of the family. In addition, sexual abuse even occurred in my intimate relationships as an adult. Moreover, I obtained a master's degree in counseling, so I was able to learn objectively that so many of my self defeating thoughts and actions were directly related to my sexual abuse experiences. As a result, I too struggled with the question, "Will I ever be happy?" A "Yes" response eluded me for years, even after multiple therapists, support groups, books, magazines, journals, conversations and tears shed with other survivors.

I now know happiness eluded me for so many years because I did not know how to find it. For over thirty years I was caught up in the pain associated with having been sexually abused as a child. I was caught up in my confused thinking and in my resulting actions for too many years. I really thought the happiness would somehow present itself to me as soon as I finished reading a particular book, or, as soon as I finished a therapy session, or as soon as I finished my college degree, or got married, or had children, or as soon as I got my big break. Well, all of those things happened in my life, and I was still unhappy. Survivors like to think that if we just work hard enough, strive hard enough, accomplish enough on the outside, then happiness will come. Other survivors don't have the energy to do all of the above, so they choose self-destructive means, still hoping that one-day happiness will arrive.

Eventually all of us realize happiness will not just arrive on its own. Once a survivor realizes all of her efforts were for naught, that's when the question, "Will I ever be happy?" returns. That's also the time when survivors realize we don't know how to get the happiness we deserve and desperately desire.

The purpose of this book is to share with you what I truly believe is the essence of what survivors need to understand and do in order to expedite obtainment of happiness in their lives. The contents of this book are the result of countless interviews with incest and child sexual abuse survivors, personal research, having developed and facilitated incest and child sexual abuse survivor support groups, work as a life coach for survivors, and my personal experiences as a survivor. I believe if survivors understand exactly what I have outlined, they will find the happiness they truly deserve.

This book is for male and female survivors alike. You will notice, however, that most of my references are related to women. This is because for most of my career I have worked directly with women and not as often with men. I have learned, however, that male survivors share many of the same issues as women. Additionally, men have another challenge to their recovery that women do not. Specifically, men have to combat the whole notion of a challenged masculinity when they have been sexually abused. I don't want my male readers to be turned off by my female references because the information in this book will help you also.

I have divided the book in three sections: The Acceptances, So What's A Trigger? and The Promises and Permissions. I have written the book so you can start anywhere you want. Just go to a particular section of interest, and you will find the information you are looking for. I tried to write the book in a simple format for ease in reading and interpretation, which is why you won't find footnotes and references throughout. I have included, however, a detailed bibliography and resource list at the end of the book for you to use as you continue your journey to happiness.

Always remember, "There *IS* Happiness After Incest and Child Sexual Abuse."

THE ACCEPTANCES
The Building Blocks To Happiness

CeCe Norwood

THE ACCEPTANCES
The Building Blocks To Happiness

As a survivor myself and as a survivor who has dedicated her life to helping other women and men overcome the devastating effects of having been sexually abused as a child, I have come to understand that there are certain concepts *we must accept as true* if we are to begin and successfully complete our journey to the happiness we deserve. I have coined these concepts "The Acceptances." I consider The Acceptances the foundation that must be set and understood before true happiness can be obtained. Of course, a foundation is the very thing all physical structures must securely and confidently sit upon whether it is a single story house or the tallest building in the world, in order for the structure to stand. Without a secure and confident foundation, the structure will most assuredly fall to the ground and have to be rebuilt. Likewise, positive childhood experiences can be considered the foundation needed for an individual to become a successful, emotionally secure adult. Being a victim of incest and/or child sexual abuse causes a shaky foundation upon which an individual's life is built. Therefore, if survivors don't utilize The Acceptances as the new foundation upon which to rebuild our lives, we will forever figuratively topple over and constantly be in a lifetime mode of rebuilding.

The Acceptances represent those issues survivors struggle with for years because we don't want to accept them as true, but yet they stand like a mountain between our deserved happiness and us. When first offered the concept of The Acceptances, most survivors don't want to accept them. They don't want to accept them because they are not pleasant. They are not pleasant because many represent facts about our life that distinguish us from those who have not been sexually abused. Other Acceptances represent serious and important changes we must make in our lives or depict ways in which we must handle our daily lives and relationships that non-survivors don't have to consider. Yet, The Acceptances are the foundational or core issues that if you believe and accept as true, you will experience a burst of clarity, energy, and strength, for perhaps the first time in your life. It's true! Common responses from survivors believing The Acceptances are, "I wish I had known about them before," and, "I wasted so many years." Embracing The Acceptances will decrease the amount of time needed for you to find the happiness you deserve. Build your solid foundation once and for all!

Don't waste any more time resisting The Acceptances.

14

Accept the fact that EVERYTHING and ANYTHING you have done to survive and get to this point in your life was necessary.

Years ago I read a book by Melba Wilson entitled *Crossing the Boundaries.* Ms. Wilson is a black woman who lives in Germany. Finding the book was a Godsend because I had desperately been trying to find anything I could to help me understand what I was going through as a black woman who is an incest and child sexual abuse survivor. Ms. Wilson writes about the assistance she was providing to other women through a support group. She states the first thing she tells survivors who come to the group is that,

"Whatever you have done to get here is okay." Wow! Wow is the response because as I have looked at my own efforts to recover and the efforts of the hundreds of women I have spoken to or interviewed, many have done things they would like to forget, as they are ashamed. Survivors have turned to using drugs and alcohol to excess, becoming full-fledged prostitutes, or using their bodies as if they were prostitutes. Others responded by stealing and lying to get what they wanted, becoming exotic dancers, losing themselves in religious doctrines, or becoming recluses or "wild children." Numerous others have become involved in multiple relationships or promiscuity, which resulted in multiple children, sometimes by multiple fathers. Tragically, multiple suicide attempts are all too common. Not surprisingly, others became perpetrators themselves. Engaging in any of these things is considered deviant or wrong by our society. As a result, survivors who have engaged in any of these behaviors further beat themselves up. First we beat ourselves up because of the abuse, and then we do it again because we may not have chosen the healthiest means to cope.

Others have chosen just as damaging coping skills, but on the outside they are not recognized by society as deviant. These are the survivors who have become perfectionists. Intellectually they know there is no such thing as perfection, but no one could tell this based on how these women run their lives. Everything in their lives must give the illusion of perfection . . . their appearance, their homes, their children, their partners, their work products, their lawn, their outside garbage cans, their cat, their dog, etc. They too beat themselves up. How could they not? They too have not gotten the relief they seek from their abusive experiences. Instead, they have unknowingly constructed a life of daily stress and strife. It's energy draining to constantly have to maintain a facade of, "I have it all together" when inside everything is disorganized. Perfection means control. Control is something no survivor had when abused. The perfectionist woman is attempting to gain a feeling of control over her life through her perfectionist practices in the same way other women have chosen socially unacceptable means to gain control.

What about the overachieving woman who does so to the detriment of her health and relationships? Yes, to the outside world she is perceived as a hard worker, a committed, get-the-job done type person. She holds a high profile position, but inside, she feels just as out of control, scared, frightened, and unhappy as the prostitute or alcoholic. Just like every other survivor, she cries into the wee hours of the morning because she too doesn't now how much longer she will be able to carry on at that pace.

Statistics tell us that 50-60% of survivors have in turn sexually abused someone else. Why would someone who has been abused do this to someone else when they realize how much pain it has caused them? The answer oftentimes depends on at what age the abuse was perpetrated. Sexually abusive behavior is taught! It is taught through direct experience or exposure to sexually explicit media such as movies, magazines, pictures, Internet, or even inappropriate conversations with a child. Children who abuse other children are usually only doing what was done to them. Often they don't know it is wrong or socially unacceptable. How could they? They are children who have been taught this perversion by the adults in their lives. Remember, 85%-90% of sexually abusive individuals are usually family members such as parents, older siblings, grandparents, uncles, aunts, etc. Kids are indoctrinated to do what adults tell them because adults "know what's best and adults don't lie."

Also remember that a normal part of sexual development is exploration of body parts. Remember the "doctor games" or the "you show me yours and I'll show you mine" comments of children? Well, if a child has not been abused, these "doctor games" are part of normal sexual development because two children of equal experiences are playing it. It's part of the normal recognition children eventually have that their body parts are different from those of the opposite sex. And like all children should, they want to explore this part of their world. There are no inappropriate sexual undertones or sexual intents, just natural exploration.

Sexual exposure to adults prior to the "doctor game" stage is what introduces the sexual undertones and abnormality to the situation because we no longer have two children with equal experiences. Some people mistakenly believe that a pre—or mid-adolescent child should know better. Maybe yes but also maybe no. It depends on whether someone has taught the child what is appropriate and not appropriate touch. Again, children do what was done to them and children only know what adults have told them. Children who might have some understanding that touching other kids is wrong may continue to do so anyway because their sexual abuse experience was not painful, but pleasurable and they want to duplicate the pleasure.

Is it totally this child's fault that she/he has turned into a perpetrator? I think not. I believe it still goes back to the adult who introduced the child to adult sexual behaviors. Why? Because first, that child would have never had the idea to perpetrate if she/he hadn't been abused, and second, the child would never have known the pleasure that can come from being sexually stimulated had an adult or older child not introduced her/him to this practice. Accept it or not, children are sexual beings. Their bodies, like adults will respond to sexual stimulation, and they will experience pleasure. This fact is exactly why it is difficult to convince a sexually active teen to stop having sex. No, they are not emotionally mature or responsible enough to handle the experience, but it is the sexual pleasure they are in pursuit of. The child who becomes a perpetrator needs help, not as a criminal, but as a survivor.

If you remember nothing else as you read this book, UNDERSTAND and BELIEVE that everything you have done, good, bad, or indifferent, you had to do! You had to respond as you did because if you had not, you would not be here today. You had to because YOU SUFFERED A MAJOR TRAUMATIC EVENT! Our traumatic experience of incest, and/or child sexual abuse is just as damaging as others who have withstood traumatic events such as military combat, serious automobile accident, mugging, robbery, miscarriage, loss of limb or eye, rape, natural disaster, or terrorist attack. All of these things are traumatic. Following none of these things can individuals just dust themselves off and move on without experiencing problems of adjustment. Sista, whatever your shame is, let it go! Please. **You did the best you could at the time with the information and abilities you had.** Forgive yourself; it will shorten your road to happiness.

Accept the fact that throughout your life you will probably always be affected by your sexual abuse experiences.

Now this is the Acceptance most survivors have told me "sucks." It doesn't "suck" because they disagree with me, but because nobody wants to believe her/his life will always be affected by something that happened as a child. We all want to believe that if we can just find the *one* thing that will take away our pain, our nightmares, our flashbacks, our disappointments, our feeling scared, unsettled, unfocused and our rage, we will be okay. We spend years and years and years and years and years trying out and doing different things, waiting for the effects of the abuse to go away from our hearts, minds, and daily lives, yet they still persist.

I'm sorry to have to tell you that your inability to *totally* and *fully* erase the effects of abuse from your life IS the reality survivors *must* accept if they are to achieve happiness in their lives. I can hear you saying, "But why? I was a child and I am an adult now," or "But why?" "I've been going to counseling, for years," or "But why? I am taking the prescribed medication given by my doctor who told me it would help me get rid of the pain." I hear you.

The answer is this: If you have gone to counseling and fully told the counselor your experiences, you have probably gotten one of the most popular diagnoses for incest and child sexual abuse survivors: Post Traumatic Stress Disorder (PTSD).

PTSD became well known following the Vietnam War. It was the diagnosis men and women were given after they returned home and it was obvious to therapists and family that veterans were reacting to their home environment as if they were still in combat. When a car backfired, they might hit the floor because the sound reminded them immediately of bombs and gunfire in war. Or, they continued to have awful, daydreams, nightmares and flashbacks about their combat experiences. Their relationships were oftentimes destroyed because some lost the ability to be intimate with others or their sex drive slowed or was nonexistent. Many could not hold jobs for any length of time because the symptoms of PTSD and/or their depressive episodes would not allow them to work regularly, or complete work assignments. Chalsa M Loo, PhD, and other researchers of military personnel have found that "being a minority may cause one to be more 'at risk' for PTSD." Don't some of the above military personnel experiences mimic our experiences as survivors? Of course they do. Like the military veterans, incest and child sexual abuse survivors have suffered a traumatic event.

Our lives, just like the veteran diagnosed with PTSD, will always be affected to some extent.

Believe it or not, I can hear you saying, "There is no way I can continue to live like this. If I don't get some relief I am going to explode!" Before you say, "Forget it" and put this book down, let me give you the good news. The good news is that if you address the effects of sexual abuse head-on, and by head-on I mean not ignoring or covering your pain and being willing to feel really awful for an indefinite period of time, the pain will lessen each day. Depending on how debilitating your pain is right now, you may not notice the lessening right away, but it is lessening. It will lessen because you have accepted the fact your life will be affected by your abuse and you are now actively working hard to identify and manage the "triggers" that are bound to happen. It is the *not* recognizing and *not* managing of triggers that keeps us unhappy or dysfunctional for longer than we need to.

Accept the fact that the only way to get over the abuse is through it.

It's probably safe to conclude that if you are a survivor reading this book you have already discovered that conscious avoidance of your child sexual abuse has not been helpful. Too many of us have been indoctrinated to believe that in hard times if we would just "be strong" or "give it over to God" or engage ourselves in continuous activities, the effects of being abused will slip away in time. So when the thoughts and feelings creep back into our consciousness, we begin to doubt our personal strength and fortitude. We begin to believe that the God of our choosing has abandoned us, or we add more commitments to our lives by saying "yes" to anyone who asks with the distorted rationale that if we are busy we won't have time to think. If you are a survivor, you personally know avoidance tactics don't work over time. In fact, the thoughts and feelings, when they return, do so with a vengeance.

It is a proven fact within the field of psychology that the primary way to get through a traumatic event is to acknowledge the severity of the event and be willing to express and feel the subsequent emotions. As survivors of incest and child sexual abuse, we have experienced a traumatic event! We have experienced the same level of trauma as a soldier in combat, or a victim of a terrorist attack, or a survivor of a horrific automobile accident. Most survivors of these major traumatic events cannot rise from their beds the morning after and continue on with their lives as if nothing has happened. Many try. Many will say, "I'm fine," or "This is not going to take over my life," or "This will not ruin my life." Some who are spiritual will say, "There must be something else I'm supposed to do with my life or otherwise I would have died." Still others will say, "It really wasn't that bad because I could have been hurt worse." What each of these responses ignores is that even though we can convince ourselves consciously, our unconscious mind still knows the full ramifications of what has happened. This is why when people are "still" or it's quiet or if there are no distractions, our real feelings surface without our permission. Some survivors have discovered this fact, so they avoid sleeping, or being alone, or being without a 24-hour a day event schedule. They are, perhaps, consciously running from their unconscious mind, which will show them their true reaction to a traumatic event every time. Our unconscious mind shows us, through our daydreams or nightmares, or panic attacks, or anxiety attacks, or our overall blah feeling that we are in distress.

In many cultures, and I know firsthand in the African American culture, it is expected that women take on a superwoman persona. This superwoman persona dictates that if your world caves in, you will get up, dust yourself off, gather your kids, find a new residence, and go home and cook dinner just like you did the day before. A superwoman does not succumb to any adversity. In fact, she is not even supposed to have any debilitating residuals. If she does, the culture says she is weak. And being perceived as weak in some cultures is unacceptable. Because some women are raised with this cultural norm, they don't feel they have any options. You can't even talk with your best friend too often about the situation if she has been raised with the same cultural expectations. Otherwise, you may feel she thinks you are weak. It's common for best friends to say, "Girl, you need to move on," or "Girl, that was so long ago; why are you still trippin' on it?" When these words are heard, the survivor further retreats and her "weak" status is confirmed. Nobody wants to be thought of as weak, so what she does is continue running from her true emotions in hopes they won't catch up with her. To avoid her true emotions, she resorts to self-defeating or self-destructive activities such as drugs, drinking, over-committing, perfectionist behaviors, etc. These things may seem to work for a month, six months, or for years, but all roads lead back to the original trauma. The *only* road to the happiness you deserve is to tell someone the whole and complete story, including the associated emotions! The *only* road to the happiness you deserve is to acknowledge that with every event you experience, you experience the event and the feelings that come with it. We can try to separate the two, and most survivors try to because the emotions can make them feel so bad, but it only prolongs the inevitable. The inevitable are the triggers that occur in our lives that cause us to re-live our sexual abuse even when we don't want too.

Believe me when I tell you once again, that the only way to get *over* your abuse is *through* it. We get through it by facing it head-on and not by avoiding or minimizing the events or the emotions.

Accept the fact that as you journey to your happiness, your personal relationships will be affected. Some will go away.

I hope you have an understanding, secure partner because you are not always going to be "present" in the relationship. How can you be if you are truly and intentionally trying to deal with your sexual abuse issues head-on? During this time, it is often not possible to consistently give emotionally in relationships that are naturally expecting much in return. Because we are in inner turmoil, we often fall short of other people's expectations and consequently the relationship is in jeopardy. To save the relationship, we try once again to bury our abuse and inner turmoil. But, anything buried alive finds its way back to the surface and the relationship becomes conflicted again. The result is a vicious cycle that often ends the relationship anyway. We are left more broken inside because another failed relationship reminds us of the sexual abuse that started the cycle in the first place. It's hard for even the most committed partner to stick by us for what is an indefinite amount of time while we work out our issues. We can't promise our partner we will be more present in the relationship in one month or six months because we don't know. For some of us, it might take a year or two to get things right.

Now don't get me wrong. All relationships don't end during this period. Survivors just need to be realistic that theirs may, and if it does, it's not their fault. The truth of the matter is that if you are in an emotional flux, you can only do the best you can, and for some relationships it may not be good enough. Yes, the grief over the lost relationship will set us back somewhat because we need to fully grieve the loss. During this time, we have to talk to our higher power and trust it was for the best. After all, what we are trying to do is get to our authentic self, so we can't pretend or bury our abuse issues just to keep the relationship going. It just won't work in the long run. It's unfortunate there are no support groups or programs like Alanon (for family and friends of substance abusers) where partners and children can go to help them understand and support their loved one while simultaneously taking care of themselves. Partners of sexual abuse survivors are often as isolated as the survivor. Who can they talk to without betraying confidences or risk backlash from the survivor should they find out they spoke to someone else about the situation?

But if a survivor is lucky and blessed to have a partner who is truly a "thick or thin" person and allows this time, the relationship will be a hundred times better for both of you in the future. Your partner will benefit by finally having the queen she/he fell in love with and both of you will have a much stronger foundation upon which to build the relationship.

Accept the fact that you may need individual counseling or group therapy or a support group or medication or several of these along your journey to happiness.

I know in some ethnic communities such as the Black and Latino community talking about family skeletons is taboo. It's a strong taboo. I say, "Forget about it!" This taboo has kept us in pain for far too long. If you are not able or willing to talk with a counselor or therapist or psychologist or psychiatrist, join a support group of survivors or find yourself a life coach whose specialty is working with survivors. Research has proven that support groups are essential for survivors and family members. Support groups allow you the opportunity to learn that there are other people who have had similar experiences or maybe even worse experiences than yours. Support groups allow you to talk without having to explain or justify your comments or feelings because everyone in the group has had similar experiences and will likely understand. Support groups are usually free and confidential. If you are required to complete basic paperwork and there are no insurance or third party payers involved, you can attend as anyone you want. In other words, you can use another name if that makes you feel more comfortable. Support groups give you a reason to get out of your house, which is important because we tend to isolate ourselves. You can go "as you are." You don't have to dress up, put make-up on, get a haircut, or put on a smiley face. Support groups also give you an opportunity to develop new friends who truly understand you, people you can be your authentic self with. The latter point is extremely important, because being authentic or "real" is one issue survivors struggle with. "Who can I truly be open and honest with?" is a question often asked. Some survivors are tired of feeling fake or guilty because they don't spend time with people who may consider them a friend. But because they haven't identified their triggers, these survivors are often times without energy to socialize. Survivors can feel fake or guilty because we have not told people we consider close friends about this huge part of who we are.

If you decide to talk with one of the professionals I mentioned above consider the following:

❖ Depending on the community in which you reside, the chances of finding a professional who looks like you may be slim to none if you are a woman of color. Nationwide, there are few people of color who work in the mental health profession. Personally, I have received individual counseling from several Caucasian, female therapists and participated in predominately white support groups. I found each helpful and was grateful for their assistance. So be cautious about assuming that just because the therapist does not look like you she/he can't help you in some way. What made me eventually start a support group for women of color, however, is that I found white therapists were unable to help me process the cultural layer of my abuse.

A lesson I learned from one of my therapists is that not talking about your sexual abuse experiences is like burying something alive. When you bury something alive, it continues to claw its way to the surface. You can put more dirt on to cover it up, but eventually it's back to the surface again. Of course, what survivors try to bury is the pain and memories of our sexual abuse. We can go along for weeks, months, or even years, and think we are okay when a "trigger" comes along and the pain and memories are right there in our faces once again. Some of us use drugs, alcohol, promiscuity, overachievement, perfectionism, religion, etc. to cover it up, but eventually it's back to the top again. That's why, Sista, you can't keep it down . . . can't forget about it. That's why no matter how much alcohol you drink or drugs you snort, when you sober up, it's right there again, sometimes larger than life. That's why, Sista, you can't fully enjoy the successes you have. Your energies are divided; you are working on being successful while simultaneously being drained because of the energy it takes to keep your abuse down. That's why our relationships often times fail—we put out energy to be in the relationship and at the same time our energy is being sucked out of us as we try to keep the residuals of our abuse off of us. Our experiences were real and alive, and we can't bury them! We have to deal with them head-on, and we can do this by talking to someone openly, honestly, and omitting nothing.

❖ Don't choose a therapist based solely on your insurance. Find someone who has experience working with incest and child sexual abuse survivors. If you go outside of your insurance network, you may have to pay a little more. Consider the money an investment in your happiness. After all, we have spent money on drugs, alcohol, excessive shopping, gambling, homes, cars, vacations, etc. trying to capture our happiness. Working with survivors is a skill that has to be developed, and some therapists don't have the skills. You don't want to be spending your time and money with someone who can't give you the help you need. Ask the potential therapist what percentage of her/his practice is dedicated to working with incest and child sexual abuse survivors. This will give you an idea as to how much experience she/he has.

❖ If you choose to go to a psychiatrist, be aware that she/he may immediately want to prescribe medication. Psychiatrists are medical doctors who specialize in mental health issues. Medical doctors are trained to prescribe medications for "anything that ails you." If you are someone who is not ready to consider medication now, be prepared to refuse the prescription or choose a counselor or psychologist or life coach because legally they do not have prescription writing ability. Try not to automatically say no to taking a medication. Think about it for a while and try to separate your thoughts and feelings about it from your cultural and family influences. I say this because many survivors automatically say no to taking a medication only because it is not culturally acceptable when in fact some type of medication might be what is needed to get through the darkest hours. If the psychologist or counselor refers you to a psychiatrist for medications, be aware this person will take you through their evaluation process. Don't assume your therapist has told the psychiatrist your story. In fact, they can't unless you sign a release. And even if you give permission for the two to discuss your situation, the psychiatrist will still do an independent evaluation so she/he can assign you a diagnosis. Independent evaluation means you will have to tell the psychiatrist your story.

❖ If you don't have insurance, there are a few facilities in all cities that have qualified therapists whose fees are on a sliding scale. Sliding scale means you are charged based on your income or ability to pay. The challenge with these facilities is that they are usually community mental health agencies that oftentimes have more people needing their services than staff to provide the service. As a result, you may have to wait a few weeks to get your first appointment and might have difficulty getting scheduled consistently with the same therapist. If you can't be guaranteed you will see the same therapist, I would go somewhere else. As you know, it's difficult enough telling your story the first time so the idea of telling a different person virtually each visit is intolerable and usually not productive. It's not productive because you usually have fifty minutes for a session, and if you repeatedly have to spend thirty minutes or more telling your story to get the new therapist "caught up," when do you get to the help you need to process the events? By the time you can, the session is over.

Accept the fact that as you journey to recovery in the early days, the physical, mental, and emotional pain will be so bad you may feel like running away or killing yourself. Don't! It's part of the journey.

Have you ever felt like bolting our your front door and running down the street until you can't run any more? Usually when people feel this way, they are totally overwhelmed. They don't feel they can take one more thing going wrong. And these are folks who were not sexually abused as children but just regular ol' folks who are overwhelmed with life's responsibilities. Survivors feel this way also, usually more intensely. In addition to managing everyday adult responsibilities, we are emotionally depleted. When you are emotionally depleted, problem solving and coping skills are almost nonexistent. Changing a light bulb feels like climbing Mount Everest. There is no energy to remember where the extra light bulbs are, go and get one, remember where the step stool is, go and get it, climb up the stool, screw out the blown bulb, screw in the new, climb back down the step stool, throw away the blown bulb, and put the step stool away. Just the thought of it, not to mention the doing, involves more energy than what is available. Consequently, survivors live with many things undone. Of course, if the survivor were in a different frame of mind and emotionally stable, the whole bulb experience would be completed in less than five minutes.

Contemplation of suicide is a common theme amongst incest and child sexual abuse survivors who have lived this type of life month after month, year after year. Attempting suicide is also common. I am hopeful that if you are an individual who has contemplated or attempted suicide, you receive some solace in knowing that you are not the only survivor who has thought about it. Most individuals will not initially talk about their thoughts or attempts of suicide but will describe how they feel as depression, which many find more socially acceptable to utter.

If you think about the traumatic event that survivors have experienced, oftentimes at young ages, it makes sense that suicide would be considered an option to relieve ourselves of the horrific physical, emotional, and mental pain that is often experienced on a daily basis. Physical pain shows itself as a psychosomatic response to the internal turmoil that is being suffered. In other words, when the mind is sick the body will follow.

Women who have been forced to perform orally will complain about their throat hurting, an inability to swallow food comfortably, and/or a sour stomach. In my work, women have reported that in response to these feeling they may eat an excessive amount of peppermints or breath mints or they always have a bottle of mouth wash or toothpaste handy so they can quickly rinse out their mouths to rid themselves of the feelings or tastes they are experiencing from their mouths, down their throats, and into their stomachs.

I have talked with some women who have experienced extreme chest pain for which they have sought medical help, thinking they were having a heart attack. Other women's skin breaks out in rashes, pimples, dry skin or excessively oily skin. Unfortunately, some women have suffered serious injury to their genitalia, rectum or vagina that causes ongoing physical pain. Some will describe an overall heaviness to their body that is not attributed to excessive body weight.

Physical pain can also manifest itself in women who shower or bathe excessively. There are women I have met who use bathing and/or showering as a way of relieving their stress. Some will report bathing or showering to the point they have stripped their skin of any natural oils and as a result also have conditions related to excessively dry skin. Other women who have reported the hot water temperature is so hot steam rises from the bath water, yet they feel no physical discomfort.

When you add these ongoing physical symptoms to the emotional pain and mental confusion that results, many, many women feel overwhelmed and as a result have considered suicide as a way of ending the intense pain. When survivors have talked about, thought about, or attempted suicide, it's really not because we genuinely want to die. Rather, it can be a statement to let anyone who is listening know and feel the intensity of her/his pain. Thoughts, feelings, and attempts of suicide mean, "I don't know how to get rid of this pain. I have tried everything I know. I don't want to feel it any more." Just like any other survivor of trauma who is shown a way to get through the pain they feel, the survivor is usually willing to do whatever it takes. Accept the fact you may experience some of the above, but don't kill yourself and don't harm yourself. When you are at your wits end and you allow yourself to experience the emotions related to having been sexually abused, you will experience a "pressure release" that will allow you to begin your walk down your road to happiness. Remember, your feelings of suicide, physical pain, and emotional pain is part of the journey to your deserved happiness and *not* the destination.

Accept the fact that as you journey, you will feel scared, unsettled, unfocused, unloved, misunderstood, overwhelmed, sick, enraged, and everything you ever thought you knew, you don't. This is also a part of the journey.

Like most survivors of any traumatic event, the survivor usually does not understand nor feel the full impact of her experiences until some time passes. Often the impact is gradual, similar to a sporadic rain that works its way into a tornado. The rain represents the first recognition that you are not okay. Maybe you are having flashbacks, you feel physically sick, or emotionally upset. As the rain becomes more intense and things begin to darken, this is when you begin to feel more and more unsettled. This is the rationalization and the minimization phase survivors often times go through as we try to make sense out of what our minds and bodies are telling us. Of course, our minds and bodies are telling us that we have been assaulted and violated and it was wrong! At the same time we are acutely aware that the assault and violation was done by someone we had unquestionably trusted. There is a battle that ensues between these two contrasting thoughts and feelings with the latter being the most perplexing. How could someone so close to us cross the invisible but ever present line between adult and child? Added to the confusion are the psychological, emotional, and intellectual games that are played upon our youthful minds, such as acting like it didn't happen, or being made to believe that we are responsible for taking care of the perpetrator, or being convinced that we are on the same level as our mother and other adult women, or being flooded with money, gifts, or privileges as evidence of our elevated status. And what about the feelings the survivor may have of enjoyment from the acts or the feeling that they were a "willing participant?" Now we are truly in the tornado and everything is dark. Our minds and bodies are filled with mixed emotions, thoughts, and behaviors. Did it really happen? Did I cause it? Will he/she really hurt or kill my family. Kill me? Will I get in trouble if they tell someone, as threatened?

As time passes we realize all of what we are experiencing will not just go away with time. As a result of this realization, anger followed by rage soon finds us. We may begin to become dysfunctional in how we handle these feelings. We choose ways to self-medicate or we become super women. Both are equally devastating because neither represents what we must truly do which is to recognize and accept that our feelings of being out of control, confused, overwhelmed and unable to think clearly are part of the journey to happiness

Accept the fact you will have to share the COMPLETE details of your sexual abuse at least once. Three times would be better.

For many women who read this Acceptance, their response is "No way. I can't. I don't want to talk about it because talking about it makes me feel worse." Well, I'm sorry to say, Sista, that if you are to achieve your deserved happiness, you must tell the COMPLETE details of your sexual abuse experience. I say three times because usually the first couple of times we omit details consciously and/or unconsciously, and ALL details need to be voiced if you are to move closer to happiness.

And yes, you will probably feel bad or even worse than ever when you do this initially because it will feel like a damn bursting. You will probably feel worse because talking will mean you will re-experience the abuse in some way. For many of us, the re-experience will mean tears will flow, our bodies will hurt, anger and rage will surface, and sadness will likely follow. I hear you saying, "And that's exactly what I don't want to happen. I'm tired of feeling bad." Think about it this way. Up to now you may not have told anyone the *complete* details, and you still feel bad. So, isn't it fair to conclude that you tried not talking about it as a way of feeling better, and it didn't work? So why not try something different?

I know you have heard the cliché that the true definition of insanity is doing the same thing over and over and expecting different results. In sexual abuse, many survivors have felt they were losing their minds and feared they would have a mental breakdown. You have to do something different! Why is talking to someone else so important? It is through talking that oftentimes we can answer our own questions or concerns. There is something about bringing voice to our heart that brings clarity to even the most complicated issues. It is through talking with someone else, we can reduce a mountainous feeling down to a molehill. I promise you that with each time you tell your complete story you will feel better and better. Talk to someone Sistas!

Accept the fact your family, partner or closest friend may never respond or react in quite the way you need them to nor when you need them to. You may have to construct a new family.

I have learned from speaking with hundreds of women that it does not matter how awful their childhood, most still morn the loss of the family society says we should have had and we spend large parts of our lives trying to construct our fantasy family life. Usually, survivors don't immediately jump to the constructing a new family phase. Before this sad revelation there is an undying hope that their birth family will deal with the sexual abuse openly and honestly and the result will be the perfect, loving, family or at least the family they had prior to the abuse. Many survivors have spent countless years trying to divulge the secret to their family or spent years trying to get their family to even acknowledge the sexual abuse occurred. For families who do try to deal with the sexual abuse, seldom does their response time or comments or methods of support or voiced understanding give the survivor what she needs at the time she needs it. It's as if they don't continually think about the abuse as we do. This is the point when many survivors understand firsthand the meaning of the cliché, "sometimes love just isn't enough."

Lucky is the survivor who has a family that is brave enough, to be supportive even if the support is clumsily offered. Those who have families who immediately deal with the perpetrator and take care of the survivor seem to have a smoother journey to happiness because they have heard or seen in action the five critical words: "It was not your fault." It's being believed and supported that makes the difference.

For Sistas who are not lucky or blessed to have a supportive family, constructing a new family becomes critical. We have to do this because we cannot recover without support. Sometimes the newly constructed family involves "borrowing" someone else's mother, father, siblings, or extended family. Or the constructed family is new friends developed from your support groups or fellow survivors. Constructing a new family, even though it may be necessary, is hard because it is excruciatingly painful to realize and accept the fact your family of origin can't or won't be of help to you. Admittedly, constructing a new family adds another layer to our abuse experiences we must get through. It's a thick layer because it requires we mourn the loss of the family that was our birthright. It may mean no contact or guarded contact with our blood relatives.

Not contact means the loss of all family traditions or normal family experiences such as graduations, birth, celebrations, deaths, etc. It means the loss of our ability to share our life experiences with the very people all of society says should be there for us. It means our children do not have a grandmother, grandfather, uncles, aunts, cousins etc. as well.

Guarded contact, although better than no contact, makes us feel like we are "on the outside of our family looking in." We can feel the tension when we are around the family. We don't really feel a part of the family anymore. There is no "homey" feeling because the conversations and interactions are superficial. We're not invited to many family functions.

For too many survivors, their family of origin is essentially dead to them. You must develop new friends and family if you are to be truly happy.

Accept the fact a belief in a higher power WILL help you through your darkest and brightest times.

When I first developed this Acceptance it didn't dawn on me that some people wouldn't understand that I was not referring to a religious deity such as God, Allah, or Buddha, or Jehovah. Because I do not want to leave out the women who are atheists or do not believe in a "God," I offer the following clarification. For some women, of course, God, Allah, or Buddha, or Jehovah, is their higher power. Typically, people who are connected to a 12-step program understand that "higher power" simply means a power greater than you.

When I worked in substance abuse treatment, finding a higher power was extremely difficult for many people until they realized a higher power does not have to be a religious deity, but just a power greater than you. Consequently, some people chose inanimate objects, or an oak tree, or an individual who is living a life of recovery as their higher power; Some eventually chose a religious deity to be their higher power, some did not, but those who continued to tell the truth and work through their issues, found their happiness and a life of recovery.

The root of this Acceptance is this: people will fail us. Good intentioned people such, as our close friends, partners, church family, family members, etc. will fail us. Why? Because they are people, people who have their own lives, problems, issues, jobs, etc. They want to be there for us, but what about at 3 a.m.? Or what about four days in a row for an hour or two or three each day? For most people, the amount of time we might need to vent, cry, repeat ourselves, or be enraged is more than they can accommodate. It's not that they don't want to or don't love us; logistically it's just not possible. For some, they care about us so much that they can't bear to hear the depth of our pain. Besides being a listening ear, which we desperately need, they don't have the answer or hug that will cure our pain.

So what can we do to get through the rough moments or extended time periods? That's where your religious deity or higher power comes in. Your higher power is the one you will speak to at 3 a.m. The one you will speak to four days in a row. The one you will yell at, scream to, cry with, and ask to help you through your pain. Your higher power is always available to you. Your higher power never minimizes your pain. Never tells you, "It happened when you were a child, so just forget about it." Your higher power never judges you. Never says you must forgive your perpetrators in order to move on with your life in happiness. Your higher power always has time. Your higher power, by virtue of listening to you, will help you get closer to claiming your happiness. Begin to depend less on people and more on your higher power for your immediate and future help. Find a higher power you can call on. By doing so, you will move closer to your deserved happiness.

Accept the fact your journey to happiness may take years of consistent work. Why shouldn't it? You suffered a major trauma.

What all survivors want is for their pain and anguish to end now! Now! This is perfectly understandable. We live in a world where many things can happen now . . . drive through restaurants and banks, speed dialing, IM, text messaging, fax, e-mail, etc. We are indoctrinated in our society that with enough time, energy, the right equipment, or enough money, virtually anything can be a "rush delivery." Unfortunately, when the "rush delivery" deals with a traumatic experience and the resulting emotions, I'm afraid what we are left with is "snail mail." In other words, our relief will get to us when it gets to us. Not a moment sooner.

I too, for years, prayed and cried relentlessly for relief from the overwhelming burden the abuse experiences had placed on my total being. But it was not until one day, without my even paying attention, the excruciating pain was gone. In fact, that same day I wrote a short paper entitled, "The Pain Is Gone Now." Now, don't get me wrong; I was still troubled by my abuse experiences but the excruciating and debilitating pain was gone. I suddenly became able to see the future; I could find humor again; I smiled more freely, and I no longer wanted to die. It took a long time . . . years.

In hindsight, I realize that had I known about The Acceptances, happiness would have been mine a lot sooner. I would not have spent so many years trying to avoid and not believing The Acceptances. Had I only known that it was going to take some time, more time than I had planned or wanted, had I only known how being sexually abused as a child affected me to the core, how it broke my spirit and how powerfully it negatively impacted my thinking and emotions, I would have probably settled down for the journey, versus resisting so much. But, I too, am a product of the "rush delivery" generation.

That's why I now describe surviving incest and child sexual abuse as a journey. A journey is ongoing. Along the journey to happiness there is pain, heartache, self analysis, self destructive behaviors, self doubt, counseling, support groups, journaling, reading, writing, crying, loneliness, poor decisions, failed relationships, etc. But all of these things are a part of the journey, not the destination! The destination point is happiness. What happens to survivors is that when we get tired of the journey, or when the journey gets too emotionally tough or we lose hope, we stop our journey by not dealing with recovery head-on. And when we stop working on our recovery, we begin to believe the journey is how things will be forever. We begin to believe that our life will always be filled with pain and dissatisfaction. This is not true! That's why another Acceptance is "Accept the fact that as you journey to recovery in the early days, the physical, mental, and emotional pain will be so bad you may feel like running away or killing yourself. Don't! It's part of the journey."

Remember, there *IS* Happiness after incest and child sexual abuse!

Accept the fact you will have to totally reprogram your thinking.

So many times I have heard survivors say, "I wish I could just wipe this whole experience out of my mind." When they say this I know exactly what they are talking about because sometimes dealing with the residuals of having been sexually abused is so overwhelming that the thoughts and feelings of it can take over your daily and even moment-to-moment thinking. It is not surprising when some survivors describe feeling a heavy weight, almost like that of a refrigerator, on their bodies the moment they open their eyes in the morning. How can you consider yourself to have a life when you awake in the morning and throughout the day you can't concentrate on the tasks at hand because of being distracted by memories of your abuse? You can have the life you want; you just have to reprogram your thinking.

The uses of the word "reprogramming" for some may make you automatically think about brainwashing. This is definitely not what I am talking about. I'm talking about reprogramming our thinking process as a conscious way of thinking differently. I'm talking about choosing to "flip the script" on ourselves. I'm talking about choosing to STOP negative, non beneficial and devaluing thoughts the moment they enter your mind. This can be done if we train ourselves to do this. It is a type of re-training ourselves to think in ways that benefit us. Reprogramming involves doing something different than what you might automatically do otherwise. And whenever we choose to do something different, there is a "learning curve" involved before it can become incorporated into our daily existence. Meaning, it may take a while before you master this skill.

There has been some research done that suggests that as much as 85% of most people's thinking is negative. And these are not necessarily incest and child sexual abuse survivors or people who have sustained any other particular trauma. Just regular folks and still 85% of their self-talk is negative. Since survivors have plenty of negative things they can think about, you have to believe our negative self-talk is probably 200%, if that's possible.

I call my negative self-talk the ""itty-bitty committee"". This "itty-bitty committee" would sit on my right shoulder and always seemed to be convening. This committee was always talking and deciding and interpreting my realities. Unfortunately, this "itty-bitty committee" many times caused me to make a decision and then back away from a decision. This committee has caused me to doubt my abilities, my strengths, my feelings, my interpretations of situations, and even my decision to want to stop the residuals or after effects of my incest and child sexual abuse from ruining my every day existence and even the remainder of my life.

"Itty-bitty committee's are powerful because there are so many members and only one of you. The membership in the committee seems to change. Sometimes the committee members are parents who were not supportive, supervisors who were jerks, children who were not appreciative, ex-lovers who were abusive, and of course, the perpetrators themselves. The committee is a solid force because they have all agreed in one way or another that you are not of value and that you will always be in turmoil following your sexual abuse experiences. "So what's the point of doing anything different?" they say or "what's the point of hoping, wishing, or praying the pain will ever end?" "What's the point of thinking that one day you will no longer be clinically depressed because you always will?" This committee is powerful!

All survivors have some form of an "itty-bitty committee". This is why some have chosen deviant ways to quiet the committee with drugs or alcohol or promiscuity or perfectionist means. It's that damn committee that speaks loudly to us daily. They talk so much until eventually we can be fooled into believing that what they are saying is reality.

The only way to get out from under the power of your "itty-bitty committee" is to *consciously* take back control of your thoughts. This means that the moment you even smell the hint of a negative thought, you immediately shut it down. You can shut the "itty-bitty committee" down by simply invoking a positive thought. To shut it down you just can't mentally think a positive thought; you have to voice a positive thought. If you are around other people, you may have to mumble a positive thought to yourself; it just has to be audible for you. Remember, you don't have to believe the positive thought at the moment, but say it anyway. Experience has also taught me that, depending on the day or mood, just voicing a positive thought may not work. If that's the case, try turning on upbeat music you like real loud or at least loud enough that you drown out the "itty-bitty committee". You see, at least for me, the "itty-bitty committee" does not have the ability to talk loudly; so high volumes wipe their voices out quickly. Sometimes before you know it, you will be singing to the music and the committee is quieted. Music is therapy! Another strategy is to simply change what you are doing. We can't change our feelings, but we can certainly change our thinking, and we can change what we are doing. For spiritually based survivors, repeating a prayer or chanting is also helpful. Here again you are not discounting your feelings, but you are changing your thoughts to more productive ones. At my lowest point I used to repeat the Hail Mary prayer over and over and sometimes faster and faster. It may sound weird, but what you are doing is bombarding your brain with the thoughts you want to have. This practice leaves no room for other thoughts as our brains can only process one thing at a time, albeit rapidly! Either of the above strategies allows you to acknowledge you are not feeling mentally or emotionally spry, but you don't have to stay that way.

As you can see, it may take some time for you to learn how to reprogram yourself from succumbing to the habit of spiraling down into sadness or depressive thoughts. It requires that instead of trying not to think about what you are feeling, you actually pay attention to what you are feeling and thinking so you can "flip the script" or change your thoughts immediately. This is a different approach, I know. But happiness is a choice and a conscious decision. Happiness does not just happen, we have to create it.

Accept the fact there may come a time when you need to be alone, not lonely, to find your true, authentic self.

Just the thought of being alone can make some survivors panic. Panic ensues because the immediate reaction is fear. Fear arises because for some survivors, the perpetrator would only sexually abuse them when they were alone. There didn't have to necessarily be any interaction with the other people, but the survivor knew that as long as people were around, no abuse would occur. Having other people around can become a shield or form of protection. Consequently, without even realizing it, a survivor constructs her adult life so people are always around. This can take the form of having the "party house" where all are welcome any time of day or night, or maybe you become the "party girl" because people know you based upon the clubs you frequent or the endless social events you attend.

Other survivors feel fear because being alone means being alone with their thoughts and feelings, and they don't want that. The distorted conclusion, therefore, is if I'm not alone, then I can't think. If I can't think, then I won't feel. If I don't feel, I won't hurt. Incest and child sexual abuse survivors are masters at making sure feelings don't get through. The problem with this approach is that even when we want feelings to get through, they don't. As a result, the relationships we do want fail. The second problem with this approach is that it is in direct opposition to what survivors should do to get to their happiness.

Most survivors miss the part of the Acceptance where I write *"alone, not lonely."* As survivors we must have "alone" time so we can be with our feelings and thoughts, so we can have time to identify our triggers, So we have time to develop "trigger buster" strategies. The longer we run from our thoughts and feelings, the longer it takes to get to our happiness. The *only* road to happiness is *through* the thoughts and feelings! We need dedicated time because the road is rocky, sometimes painful and confusing. We won't be lonely because we know we need to involve ourselves in a support group, so we do. We know we may need to see a therapist, so we do. We are reading books, articles, or journaling to help ourselves. We are working, attending school or involving ourselves in important activities so we have opportunity to be around other people. They are just not in our personal space. We may initially "feel" lonely, but in reality we are just physically alone.

I know some of you are screaming, "And what am I supposed to do with my kids?" Our relationships with our children are obviously a different type of emotional investment than with a partner. Trying to simultaneously raise kids and deal with having been sexually abused is tough. It is oftentimes the negative effects of our sexual abuse impacting our relationship with our children that becomes the driving force for some survivors to start addressing their issues head-one.

Survivors who are mothers are often guilt-ridden because they recognize they are not fully "present" with their children. It's difficult, if not virtually impossible, to care for your children the way you want to or know you need to when you are depressed, depleted of emotional energy, or constantly fearful someone will sexually abuse your children.

Children need their mothers for daily living as well as emotional support and love. We know this all too well, and some of us have fallen short. Knowing they have fallen short has caused many women to spiral down even further into sadness or depression. Our mothering ability or perceived lack of it becomes something else we beat ourselves up about.

I recall a 27 year old, married, stay at home mother, named Shari who shared she realized one day her 2 ½ year-old son was not developing language skills. As an educated woman she knew it was because she was not talking to him. She said she was so depressed and overwhelmed with the memories and feelings of the sexual abuse by her brother, the strain on her marital relations with her husband, and the pressure she received from her extended family members to engage in family activities that she rarely spoke to anyone throughout the day and no one visited. Daily she found herself putting her son in a safe corner with his toys and the television. When a girlfriend inquired one day why her son was crying she immediately felt sick; it had been over five hours since she had fed him. She had totally forgotten to feed him! After that day her friend called daily to remind her to feed her son. She broke down in tears from the memory of how she had neglected her child.

I remember another support group member who shared how she did not like the fact her young children hugged and kissed her all the time. She knew she needed to reciprocate but found it extremely difficult and sometimes gently pushed them away or moved so the hug or kiss could not be completed. The closeness and emotion they needed and wanted from her was often too much for her to give. She felt sad, guilty, and like a bad mother.

Another member of the group suggested she start hugging and kissing her kids *before* they approach her because she had the same issue with her kids. She said it was not immediate, but she soon realized her reaction was because the overtures of her kids triggered the feelings she felt when her abusers made her engage in activities she didn't want to. When she started hugging and kissing her kids first, it reduced the number of times they approached her without notice. She concluded this approach gave her kids what they need emotionally; it gave her a feeling of control over her body, and it minimized her feelings that she was a "bad mother." What this woman did was recognize her kids were a trigger and then developed a "trigger buster" strategy that worked for herself and her children.

There are some survivors who don't have the energy level or mental fortitude, as the above woman, to identify that their kids may be a trigger nor do they know how to manage the resulting anxiety. As a result, they may not be "good" for their children during a particular time period. They love their kids dearly; they are just emotionally depleted. Sometimes other people recognize this, and sometimes the survivor does. What has been helpful for the kids and the survivor in this situation is for the children to live temporarily with a trusted family member or friend. This approach allows the survivor time to work out her issues without guilt, as she knows the children's daily living and emotional needs are being met. Survivors, who have been courageous and selfless enough to invoke this extreme "trigger buster" strategy still love, communicate with and see their children during this physical temporary separation. When the survivor has gotten a handle on things, the kids return to a healthy, nurturing environment.

Having a partner can also be the answer to, "What about my kids?" Your understanding partner may have to become the primary caregiver during those times when you need your alone time.

Alone time also means you should not be putting available energies into developing an intimate relationship with anyone new. Utilize the alone time to work on you.

If you are already in a relationship you are going to have to somehow negotiate your alone time with your partner and balance it with the energies needed to sustain a healthy relationship.

Accept the fact that everything that previously worked to keep your anxiety, memories, sadness, depression, fear, anger, etc. in control will eventually stop working. Even if you do it more.

The more incest and child sexual abuse survivors I talk with, the more I realize that a sexual abuse survivor will do just about anything to prevent the memories and pain of her abuse from reaching her conscious mind. Survivors have tried so many things. For example, many women become either prostitutes or exotic dancers. They will tell you when they first started either of these professions most were not aware their career choice might be a reaction to their sexual abuse. Rather, they'll say they got into it for the money.

In these environments there is definitely a tendency for customers to believe that given enough money the woman is required to perform on demand. It is usually only with the passing of time, repeated experiences with the male customers' sense of entitlement to their bodies and/or time that caused them to begin to look at their profession differently. Woman after woman has reported this is the point when things changed for the worse. This is when her job became one giant trigger! Unfortunately, by the time most recognize what is going on, she is dependent on the money for survival.

For a short while it works to pretend they are in control of the situation. Survivors mistakenly believe they have control because they determine what acts they will perform, how much it will cost, and how long they will do it. But eventually the pain and memories of the abuse surfaces, won't be pushed back down, and the survivor can slip into sadness, anger, depression, or possibly rage. Now the dilemma becomes how to keep the money flowing while simultaneously managing this huge trigger. Understand that usually during this time, the survivor is not thinking, "I'm being triggered, so how can I manage it." Instead they are thinking, "I feel terrible inside," and may recognize similarities between their sexual abuse feelings or memories and their career. Flashbacks during this time are common.

Most survivors don't consider drug and alcohol usage as a form of self-medicating. Ingesting drugs and alcohol initially works to clear the mind and numb the pain, but the cycle of substance abuse dictates that what it took to get high the first time must eventually be doubled or tripled in order to achieve the no thinking or no feeling state of mind the survivor wants. Considering how substance abuse, substance dependence and the effects drugs (including prescription) can have on your body, not getting "hooked" or "strung out" isn't even an option. Those who are prescription drug users must understand that they are also drug addicts if they use the drug more often than prescribed, lie to physicians about having lost their prescription bottles in order to get a new script, buy their drugs from an individual, and/or go to different doctors to get the same prescription. Too many survivors have become drug addicts or alcoholics and stay in addiction for years. Now they have two problems: trying to recover from being sexually abused and trying to recover from substance abuse at the same time. If the survivor is the primary caregiver, she has a third problem because she must also take care of her children. Some survivors who are addicted to substances can get fooled into thinking that if they get their substance abuse handled, recovery from being sexually abused will automatically follow. Wrong! It doesn't work that way. Each one has to be dealt with individually. In fact, truth be told, the sexual abuse issues probably started first and the addiction followed because many of us have used substances as a "trigger buster" strategy. So, in order for you to sustain a life free of drugs and alcohol, you first have to deal with the root cause, the sexual abuse. Deal with your sexual abuse and recovery from the substance abuse will follow.

The survivor who takes psychotropic medication without some type of "talk therapy" should consider discontinuing this practice. Taking more medication(s) for a longer period of time is not the answer for the majority of survivors I have had contact with. After a while, when the medication reaches its peak efficacy and it doesn't seem to "work" any more, it still comes back to facing your incest and child sexual abuse issues head-on because you are no closer to your happiness, only more time has passed. The general idea of taking medication is to help calm you, so with a clear mind, you can better explore the root cause of your issues. The medication itself does not resolve your issues or pain.

Some survivors have given up normal sleeping to avoid the pain. It's not that they never sleep, but rather, they cannot go to bed and fall asleep naturally. Rather, they fall asleep wherever they do in places like a couch or a chair or on the floor. They are unable to sleep throughout the night without waking up repeatedly. The goal of this type of sleeping pattern, by most reports, is to avoid the feelings associated with the dark and their perpetrator(s) coming into their bedroom uninvited. It also avoids the quiet time of night when people are trying to fall asleep and their thoughts won't stop. I have met women who have slept in this way for years. The end result is fatigue, exhaustion, body aches, and the pain of the abuse continues. It continues because the reason for this dysfunctional sleep pattern is not dealt with.

Food is another strategy survivors use to numb themselves, and the result of excessive eating is used as a shield or form of protection. Food seems to work initially for a couple of reasons. First, the preparation time in the form of cooking for yourself or going through your favorite drive thru is a time filler. It puts something else on your mind for that short period of time. Second, eating your favorite food may even give you a sense of excitement and pleasure. The end result of too much food, of course, is gaining weight or at its extreme, obesity.

Considering that we live in such a weight and appearance conscious society, most people would never consider that someone would intentionally put on weight. But survivors often do. The distorted logic in this approach is that if I am overweight, then no one will want me. If no one wants me, I won't be approached and have to deal with the triggers that will likely follow. The mistake in this logic is that there are plenty of suitors in the world who prefer and love full-figured women. Therefore, survivors are still approached by people who find them attractive and as a result are triggered anyway. Why is someone pursuing a survivor a trigger? For some survivors, no matter how appropriately they are approached, the initial reaction can be fear or the question, "What do you want?" The overture can also remind a survivor of how much she wants a close, intimate relationship with someone while simultaneously triggering her feelings of inadequacy or perceived inability to relax enough to nurture such a relationship. Others, at the time of the approach, jump way ahead to possible sexual overtures that can then enlist a myriad of emotions they want to avoid.

Sistas, you can't avoid triggers by layering your body with fat; you only compromise your health. You are a beautiful woman and no matter what your body size, some people can "see" right through to your heart and want to be in your company. Neither overeating nor undereating will ever get you what you want. You have to manage the trigger, which in this case is someone finding you attractive and interesting, and not avoid it. You are not invisible. People see you and will respond to your presence positively.

Gambling and/or shopping are also used to excess by some. Did you know that studies have shown that both of these activities release seratonin in our brains? Serotonin is the chemical that gives us pleasure. Neither gambling nor shopping in and of itself is problematic. They become a problem when we use them to avoid dealing with our survival issues. They become a problem when we are spending money we don't have because we are in pursuit, usually unknowingly, of short-term pleasure. I have interacted with dozens of women who shop for hours, some daily, and after they have purchased the items, they no longer find pleasure in them. They don't even wear or use the purchases. Purchases are just put in the closet or thrown in a corner and forgotten. Why? Because by the time you return home, the seratonin levels have adjusted, and you are left with the original gaping hole you tried desperately to fill through shopping or gambling. For some they now have two pains: the sexual abuse memories and the dread over the money that was spent.

Some survivors become sex addicts. No, they don't, necessarily, have sex for money, but they have sex as a means of trying to feel loved, needed, wanted, or to avoid being alone. We don't know this at first. Some survivors are the original "booty callers." Because we are accustomed to using our bodies, we are fooled into thinking we are in control when we make the call. We have feelings of control because some have learned how to manipulate and "work" other people by using the allure of their bodies. It usually doesn't take long, however, for old feelings of emotional emptiness to surface. Depending on how transparent the survivor is, it usually doesn't take long for the "booty call" to realize she might be an "easy mark" if they convincingly pretend to love and care about her. It doesn't matter if the survivor was the first to recognize that sex was a "filler" or the sex partner to recognize that pretending will keep the sex flowing because it's all going to blow up in the face of the survivor anyway. Survivors eventually recognize they were "looking for love in all of the wrong places" and are left empty once again.

I'm reminded of Jennifer who stated that when she was in college, away from her family and perpetrator, she realized how lonely she felt. She stated she wanted desperately to be in a loving, committed relationship but could not find anyone of interest. Being an attractive woman, she was often pursued by individuals for what she knew was only for sex. At first, she put them off. But as time went on, somewhere in her mind, she decided having someone around who only wanted sex was better than being alone. She realized that if she "worked" it right, she could postpone the sex by requiring they go to dinner, or a movie, or a walk. These activities were time fillers and gave her the illusion the "booty call" was someone of significance. She knew they were not but she would stuff those feelings down and pretend. She shared that the sex was not physically unsatisfying, but it definitely was emotionally unsatisfying. Having been abused for so long by different people, she recognized the difference between sex and making love to committed partner, but she would stuff those feelings down also. She said she found herself asking these "booty calls" during the sex act if they loved her. She knew they didn't, but she hoped they would lie so the fantasy could continue. Most said, "yes" in the heat of the passion, but she knew it wasn't so. When the sex was over, there was no cuddling or expressions of intimacy. When they left, she knew she would only communicate with them when either wanted sex again. Jennifer said she maintained this pattern throughout her college life. After a while, just like all self-destructing "trigger buster" strategies, she only ended up feeling worse about herself. She later realized she wasted time she could have been using to work through her abuse issues in a more productive way.

To get to our deserved happiness, we have to avoid behaviors that prevent us from dealing with our abuse issues head-on.

THE ACCEPTANCES

❖ Accept the fact that EVERYTHING and ANYTHING you have done to survive and get to this point in your life was necessary.

❖ Accept the fact that throughout your life you will probably always be affected by your sexual abuse experiences.

❖ Accept the fact that the only way to get *over* the abuse is to go *through* it.

❖ Accept the fact that as you journey to your happiness, your personal relationships will be affected. Some will go away.

❖ Accept the fact you may need individual counseling or group therapy or a support group or medication, or several of these along your journey to happiness.

❖ Accept the fact that as you journey to recovery in the early days, the physical, mental, and emotional pain will be so bad you may feel like running away or killing yourself. Don't! It's part of the journey.

❖ Accept the fact that as you journey, you will be scared, feel unsettled, unfocused, unloved, misunderstood, overwhelmed, sick, enraged, and everything you ever thought you knew, you don't. This is also a part of the journey.

❖ Accept the fact you will have to share the *complete* details of your sexual abuse at least once. Three times would be better.

❖ Accept the fact your family, partner or closest friend may never respond or react in quite the *way* you need them to or *when* you need them to. You may have to construct a new family.

❖ Accept the fact a belief in a higher power will help you through your darkest and brightest times.

❖ Accept the fact your journey to happiness may take years of consistent work. Why shouldn't it? You suffered a major trauma.

❖ Accept the fact you will have to totally reprogram your thinking.

❖ Accept the fact there may come a time when you need to be alone, not lonely, to find your true, authentic self.

❖ Accept the fact that everything that previously worked to keep your anxiety, memories, sadness, depression, fear, anger, etc. in control will eventually stop working. Even if you do it more.

So What's a Trigger?

How To Identify Triggers and Develop "Trigger Busters"

So What's A Trigger?
How To Identify And Develop "Trigger Busters"

A trigger is an event or experience that takes an individual immediately back emotionally and/or mentally and/or visually and/or physically to an experience. A trigger does not necessarily have to be negative. People can be triggered to remember positive experiences. Perhaps someone who is an excellent baker raised you and the smell of baked products often permeated their home. Maybe you were a part of this pleasant baking experience. Well years later, perhaps even after you had forgotten how much you loved that experience, you are walking past a bakery and the aroma hits your nostrils. You are immediately triggered back to that experience and you might even be able to visualize the kitchen, the baking process, the laugher, and the fun. Experiencing that trigger might prompt you to go into the bakery and buy a baked good when you had no prior intentions. Do you know that realtors have been known to encourage their sellers to bake something prior to prospective buyers' visits? They are hoping to trigger pleasant memories in the potential buyer of positive home experiences that will in turn influence them to buy the seller's house. Another pleasant trigger might be when you see grandmother figures and you recall the loving relationship you had with yours. You might be able to actually feel your grandmother holding you or you might start to daydream about your anticipation of being a grandmother so you can give the love you received to your grandchildren.

Triggers are everywhere. For survivors, unfortunately, our triggers are not pleasant. For example, a woman by the name of Angela who was sexually abused by her father told me one day that it was not until she married her husband did she recognize why cigarette smoking of a particular brand always bothered her. She told me her husband's practice following intimate relations was to smoke a particular brand of cigarette. When she was triggered back to her sexual abuse by her father the first time she smelled the smoke, she felt panic but she didn't know why. She loved her husband. She wanted to be sexual with her husband but, nonetheless, she noticed she avoided sexual relations with him. She didn't know why. In fact, she didn't know why until later when she had a flashback to an abuse incident. She recalled that often times when her father was sexually abusing her he would smoke this same brand of cigarettes! Fortunately, she was able to talk with her husband about it and he discontinued this practice and in fact he was relieved to know what was going on.

Another trigger might be seeing an adult male with a child sitting on his lap. Perhaps sitting on laps was part of your abuse experience so the sight of the child on the adult's lap triggers you. Or perhaps you have settled in to watch a movie and out of nowhere a sexual abuse theme is introduced. Other triggers might be related to a particular time of the year. Maybe your abuser was a family member and his/her birthday comes up. Or it's the holiday season when family gets together and you are triggered because you know your abuser(s) will be at the family celebration or possibly the holiday season in general reminds you of the family you don't believe you have because of the sexual abuse. Sometimes girls have been impregnated following their abuse, so anything related to pregnancy, child bearing or raising of children could be a trigger.

Trusting people is a gigantic hurdle many survivors have to get over so the trigger can be someone being dishonest with you directly or by omission. Someone who is trustworthy, loving, attentive, etc can also trigger us. Touch is often times uncomfortable for survivors, so an innocent touch by a passerby, or colleague, or friend, or lover can be a trigger.

If survivors have not identified their personal triggers and learn to watch out for them, the result is that we are blindsided and have no idea why we feel sad, depressed, anxious, unmotivated, unloved, unfocused, can't get out of bed, etc. At worst, we can spiral down into a deep hole filled with despair that could take us days, weeks, months, or even years to climb up out of. Some women, without help, never get out of this deep hole. For them things just keep getting worse because there is no energy or perceived ability to problem solve what is really going on. Sometimes we get fooled and think the current incident such as the innocent touch of a passerby is the culprit when it's not. In some cases we may not have even been consciously aware of the touch but we can still be affected by it because our body remembers. The incident triggered us back to our visualization and/or emotions about our abuse.

It is important to note that triggers show their ugly head gradually. You are not going to be able to identify all of your triggers at once. It doesn't work that way. It is when you begin to live your life consciously are you able to connect the dots between triggers and the abuse. In order to be triggered you must have experiences and of course experiences happen as you live. As we master the skill of living consciously we will become more and more aware of our triggers.

Now the obvious question is "after I have identified my triggers, then what?" How do you manage or "bust" a trigger? Well, I have to come up with what I call "Trigger Busters" that must be used if we are to successfully manager our triggers. The ways to manage triggers are infinite. They are infinite because they are specific to the survivor who will need many methods to manage the different triggers experienced throughout life. What may work for me to manage a trigger may not work for you. You also need to know that identifying "trigger buster" strategies is a heck of a lot easier than identifying the trigger itself. It can be easier because by the time we identify our triggers our eyes are wide open and as a result we have the ability to discern what will help us. Let me give you some universal "Trigger Buster" strategies.

❖ Talking about how you are feeling to someone else is one of the most effective "trigger busters." Not to yourself, someone else! When survivors talk to themselves, the effects of the trigger can get bigger instead of smaller. Some of this is not just because we are survivors. Remember that 85% of most people's self talk is negative. Add abuse on top of it and that percentage would probably rise to 200% quit easily. You have to be careful whom you choose to speak with. Your best friend or partner, who is not a survivor, may not be the best person even though you would earnestly say, "we can talk about anything." A better person might be a fellow survivor, counselor, or support group member. Don't assume, however, that just because someone is a fellow survivor the conversation will be productive. Whether they are the best choice will depend if they have or are dealing with their own abuse issues head-on.

Why is talking to someone else so important? Because it is through talking that often times we can answer our own questions or concerns. There is something about bringing voice to our heart that brings clarity to even the most complicated issues. It is through talking we can reduce a mountainous feeling down to a molehill. Talk to someone Sistas!

In many communities, especially ethnic communities, talking about family skeletons is taboo. These communities, just like mainstream communities, are responsible for the pervasiveness of child sexual abuse in their communities and our society because of their silence. When a community is silent about the sexual abuse of its children, it gives sexual perpetrators permission and access to the community's children. At my 8th grade graduation I received a small plaque that read, "Silence is Consent!" How true this statement is.

❖ Learn how to communicate with your higher power or whatever gives you strength. Don't worry about religious doctrines, just talk. Make up your own prayers or chants. Pray for clarity, courage, and relief from your pain. Ask for help in learning how to genuinely show love to your children and partner and to fully receive love. And ask for strength to get through the darkest part of your journey to true and complete happiness. Ask for what you need!

❖ Read daily affirmation books as a means of reprogramming your thinking. My favorite one of all is by Iyanna Vansant. I love it because each month has a particular theme, so I can concentrate on one area of my life. I have had this book now for four years and I dog-ear the daily messages that have the greatest impact on me. I am often surprised how in past years a message may not have seemed especially relevant but it speaks loud and clearly to me this year. Some survivors have multiple books they read. Read the affirmation out loud. You will be surprised how the message will sink in deeper. Consider reading the affirmation more than once during a day as another way of helping it sink it. Believe the affirmation even if you don't believe it.

❖ Write your thoughts and feelings through letters or journals. The letters don't have to be mailed and the journals don't have to be shared. The idea of writing is to give you opportunity to express yourself no holds barred. I know that many women don't like to journal because they fear someone may read the journal without permission. I know for years I wouldn't journal for this reason. Or they are concerned someone will find them after they die. In both cases, you may be right; someone might read them. In the first situation, consider putting them in a lock box or your favorite hiding place. In the latter situation, think about it, you're dead, so who cares. In fact, maybe the person who finds them will finally realize how devastating being sexually abused as a child has been to your life and will actually become an advocate for children and survivors to help eradicate this major social and health problem.

❖ Don't go places or participate in activities you don't want to. People, who are not sensitive to our journey will oftentimes encourage or put nonverbal or verbal pressure on us to attend events where the perpetrator will be in attendance or expect us at the activity just because of the type of event it is. Maybe it's a holiday or birthday, or graduation or wedding, etc. If the idea of going causes you some distress and you are unable to articulate the basis for the distress, you are being triggered and what might be best for you is to not attend the event or to put in place whatever safeguards will make you more comfortable should *you* decide to go.

At first glance this strategy might seem easy and it may be for some. Where the challenge comes in is when you may actually want to attend the event and become upset or resentful your sexual abuse experience is preventing you from attending. So rather than bust the trigger, you can succumb to it quickly. It is also challenging because you may feel extreme guilt about not attending because you know you will disappoint someone who is important to you. What some survivors have done to get over the initial guilt is to remind themselves they are an adult and can make their own choices. We have to do what is best for us! Some listen to music, watch TV, visit a friend, or journal to help them get beyond the initial feelings of guilt. Do whatever you need to do to feel okay about your decision even if others are unhappy. Don't expect to feel guilt-free the first few times you use this strategy because it takes a while. We are so conditioned to please others at our expense that it's hard to put our desires first sometimes. We must put ourselves first!

❖ Immediately remove yourself from the trigger. This may be necessary if you are someplace and the perpetrator comes in. No, you shouldn't have to leave, but if staying heightens your uneasiness, then give yourself permission to leave. Do not go home if you are concerned that by doing so you will spiral down emotionally; instead continue your fun somewhere else. As time goes on and you become expert in invoking your "trigger buster" strategies, you will find you won't be as uneasy if your perpetrator shows up and you will actually be able to stay and have a good time.

❖ Allow yourself to feel your anger, upset, hurt feelings, etc for an allotted period of time. Acknowledge you have the right to feel bad about what has happened because you definitely do. You can't control your feelings, so stop trying. You can, however, control what you do following your experience of a feeling. After your allotted time, do something else. Do something else even if you don't "feel" like it.

❖ Force yourself to get out of your bed or house every day. Don't wait until you *feel* like it; just do it! You don't have to go anywhere in particular; just change your environment. Go outside and sit on your porch or in your backyard or walk around the block or go for a drive or do a load of laundry or clean off one counter top. As survivors, if we wait until we "*feel*" like it, we usually won't do anything. If we don't do anything then we are not closing in on our deserved happiness. This is especially crucial in the early days of our recovery when we have not identified our triggers or buster strategies. We can quickly decide that because I "feel" sad, depressed, angry, listless, unmotivated, then I won't or I can't _____ (you fill in the blank). Remember, you can't change how you feel, but you can change what you think and what you do. Changes in thinking and doing will help manage the feelings or emotions.

❖ Be open to the idea of taking medication as a means of evening out your moods. Depression is known to occur because of chemical imbalances in the brain. Certain medications will level these chemicals and in turn minimize the huge mood swings some of us suffer. I know some of you think that if you take medication you are somehow a weak person, or you believe if you just tried harder you would be okay; I know I did. I now know this is not true. With depression or PTSD, Bi-Polar, etc. we're talking about a biological and/or psychological cause; therefore, they are not diagnosed because of the lack of an individual's resolve. No, the medication did not stop my triggers but it gave me a clearer, calmer mind so the swings in my mood were not as great, and as a result I was better able to identify my triggers and come up with logical "trigger busters".

The above are just a sampling of "Trigger Buster" Strategies that survivors have used successfully. Many will work for you; some may not. As you learn your triggers by living consciously you will increase your number of "trigger buster" strategies by developing your own. In many ways all incest and child sexual abuse survivors have similar experiences but many are unique, so it follows that "trigger buster" strategies will also be unique. Always remember that identifying triggers, and invoking your "trigger buster" strategies *IS* the key to maintaining your life of happiness.

THE PROMISES AND PERMISSIONS

Maintaining Your Happiness

The Promises and Permissions
Maintaining Your Happiness

Just like in any trauma recovery program, maintaining what you have learned and consistent diligence in assuring you don't backslide must be done as you continue your lifetime recovery from being sexually abused as a child. If you don't develop and work a maintenance plan you will look up one day and discover your newfound happiness has slipped away and you have reverted back to non-beneficial thinking and self-destructive behaviors.

Happiness is a choice and therefore must be chosen on a daily basis. You must realize that things are going to happen in your life that will trigger you back to your incest and/or child sexual abuse experiences. Understand that triggers are not necessarily major events; simple things can trigger a survivor, like you get sick when living alone and there is no one to take care of you, or you don't live alone and whoever you live with isn't quick enough in responding to your needs, or your car brakes down and you can't think of anyone to call for help, you get married, you graduate from school, you smell that certain smell, or you run into your perpetrator. Each of these simple life time events can take survivors back to feelings of isolation, loneliness, anger, rage, lack of genuine love, lack of family or close friends, etc. You will be "there" before you know it. When any of these things or others happens to a survivor she can be pushed back into overwhelming feelings of sadness, hopelessness, helplessness, depression, and/or a general blah feeling, etc. To help you through these inevitable times, I have developed the Promises and Permissions.

The Promises and Permissions are critical for you to remember and utilize if you are to continue experiencing life long happiness. Don't be fooled into thinking that once you feel relief from the excruciating pain that took over your life for months or years that you are somehow "out of the woods," because you are not. You will be confronted daily with triggers that will try to force you back to your old self-destructive ways of thinking and behaving. WHEN this happens (not IF this happens) refer back to the Promises and Permissions you made to yourself and you will find solace and strength to successfully manage the triggers.

The Promises and Permissions are here to help you keep things in perspective. They will help you remember that even though situations or people or events at first blush may appear to be related to our abuse experience they may not be, but are actually just part of the life experience of all humans. But, if the situation, people or events are related to your sexual abuse experiences, the Promises and Permissions will help you through.

PROMISE to remember your triggers and immediately invoke your "trigger buster" strategies.

Identifying and managing triggers is THE crux of maintaining your deserved happiness. Identification of your triggers is probably the most difficult part of the recovery process because as survivors we have spent a lifetime ignoring our mental, emotional, and body cues. We did this as a strategy to manage the pain we were experiencing. Unfortunately, we have done this so long that ignoring our cues has become an automatic response to anything we perceive as negative happening in our life. If you are to maintain your deserved happiness, you must let this survival strategy go! **You must promise yourself to live life consciously.** To do so, you have to be constantly aware of how you are feeling, when you begin to get the blahs, or when you find you are processing an event or a comment someone has made through a negative lens. The conscious awareness of yourself will allow you to immediately reprogram your thinking by putting the event into perspective followed by invoking one of the "trigger buster" strategies that works for you. By living consciously, you may find that because life involves constant problem solving, some feelings or physical responses to situations may not be related to your abuse at all but to just plain ol' living. An example of what I'm talking about might be the fact a woman's monthly cycle can mess with hormones and in turn effect her mood. If you are not consciously living, you might mistake the blahs or depressed feelings as being related to your abuse, when in fact they are just the result of a temporary chemical imbalance you are experiencing which was brought on by your menstrual cycle. With this realization, you can reprogram your thoughts to reflect the actual situation and not interpret it as an indication that your happiness is slipping away. Or perhaps by living consciously you learn that the holidays are times when you start feeling depressed or blah. When the holidays come around be aware of this fact and remind yourself, "Oh, it's the holidays; that's why I feel this way." In both of these examples, take note that I am not suggesting you ignore your feelings, because you can't, but rather acknowledge them as a trigger issue and invoke your "trigger buster" strategy so you can move, on versus slipping back.

I PROMISE to remember my triggers and immediately invoke my "Trigger Buster" strategies.

Give yourself permission to be really, really, really mad, angry, and/or enraged about being sexually abused and how it has affected your life.

Because survivors spend lots of time trying to avoid feelings, we have often tried to minimize, downplay, and ignore our anger or even rage as a way of trying to deal with the tornado of feelings we have following our incest and/or child sexual abuse experiences. In our society, too many of us have been indoctrinated that it's not nice or lady—like to be angry. Consequently, this unexpressed anger has turned into rage by the time we reach adulthood. Oftentimes the rage is turned inward and sometimes outward at other people.

We MUST give ourselves permission and times to be really pissed off at what has happened to us and how it has affected our lives. It's okay let it out! Henry Nouwen once said, "The only feelings that do not heal are the ones you hide." I agree 1000 percent. Experience the feelings and take notice as they eventually lose their magnitude and consequent power over your life.

This permission requires you to allow yourself an allotted period of time to experience and express your feelings and emotions such as sadness, disappointment, loneliness, anger, rage, etc. To successfully do this, you have to be consciously aware that you are giving yourself permission to experience these feelings and emotions *temporarily* and not allow yourself to spiral down. It is recommended you not keep your feelings and emotions swirling around in your head because anytime you keep feelings and emotions at the cerebral level, they quickly turn into a mountainous situation and they are no longer being experienced as a temporary relief valve. Meaning, if we do not express our thoughts and feelings out loud, they can somehow become a much bigger, sad, or depressive issue than what in reality it is.

It's not required that you verbally talk with someone else, although its nice if you can. Instead, you can talk aloud to yourself, talk into a tape recorder, write down your thoughts on a piece of paper you can throw away if you want, or maybe create a poem. The objective is to not stew in your emotions, but to get them outside of your head and body. For other people, a better strategy might be to do something physical. Punch a pillow; go for a long jog, or brisk walk as you talk aloud to yourself. Sometimes repeating a daily affirmation is beneficial or reciting a meaningful prayer as you bring yourself out of the "funk" can be extremely helpful. I recall in my darkest moments I would repeat the Hail Mary prayer in quick succession as a way of drowning out the negative thoughts and feelings I was experiencing at the time. I'm sure I sounded "crazy" if anyone overheard me, but this practice was extremely beneficial in relieving the oppressive feelings I was experiencing.

The point of this Permission is that even after we have obtained our happiness, we will be triggered for life. Just like during our journey to happiness we had to be conscious of how we were feeling and if necessary invoke a "trigger buster" strategy, we have to continue to do this throughout life to maintain our happiness. It is OKAY to be really, really mad, sad, disappointed or enraged. Give yourself permission to be so BUT only for an allotted period of time.

I give myself Permission to be really, really, really, mad, angry, and/or enraged about being sexually abused and how it has affected my life.

Promise to openly share your story to keep sexual abuse of children in everyone's face.

Sharing your story is a common component in trauma recovery maintenance programs. For sexual abuse survivors, openly sharing our story serves three central benefits. First, as indicated in The Acceptances chapter, "You have to accept the fact you will have to share the *COMPLETE* details of your sexual abuse at least once. Three times would be better if you are to successfully journey the road to happiness." Sharing our story gets all of those feelings out of our bodies and therefore minimizing their power.

The second advantage is that if more survivors would tell their stories, the world would be more conscious of the pervasiveness and cost incest and child sexual abuse has on the individual and our society. It appears our society continues to consider being a victim of incest and/or child sexual abuse as an individual problem, even through there is substantial research demonstrating that it is much more than an individual problem but, in fact, it is a devastating social and public health problem. If survivors, as individual members of a society, are not self-actualizing or utilizing all of their talents and skills maximally because they have been traumatized, neither can their children, their family, their community, nor the society at large be healthy and self-sustaining. Traumatized individuals find it extremely difficult to live up to their full potential.

Thirdly, telling our stories encourages other survivors to tell theirs. They can see strength and promise in our ability to speak openly. They will be encouraged to talk to someone. They understand from listening to other survivors that it can happen to anyone and they realize being sexually abused was not their fault. We have to tell our stories for the survivors who cannot yet speak. We have to tell our stories so we can maintain our happiness. Promise to openly share your story. It's imperative for you and for victims that survivors keep sexual abuse of children in everyone's face!

I Promise to openly share my story to keep sexual abuse of children in everyone's face.

Give yourself permission to tell the truth, irrespective of who will be mad. The truth will assure your happiness.

Survivors are under so much pressure to be quiet. I remember a family member mad about a newspaper article written about me and a support group I started. She yelled at me "Nobody wants this known about their family!" That is the overwhelming sentiment of almost everyone; even the families where it is openly discussed. Some survivors have been raised with the belief that family skeletons stay in the family closet, and there are serious consequences when this is breached. Others face being ostracized by friends and family should "the secret" be known. Because the idea of family is so powerful, many survivors for years keep the truth secret for the sake of the family and suffer tremendously. We suffer because it's too much to hold in. Some survivors attempt or commit suicide because they can no longer hold it in. Other survivors relegate themselves to living a life of personal hell.

If you want to change your life, you will always have to speak the truth, not to hurt, but to keep the facts straight, no matter how ugly. Doing so further validates that the abuse happened and it can't be ignored in family life. Yes, family will be mad. Some family members won't speak to you. But aren't some people already mad and some family already not speaking? So what do you gain by speaking your truth? A lot! Freedom, validation, and honor. Eventually the truth will set them free also. They're just not ready to face it.

You lose nothing by speaking out.

I give myself Permission to tell the truth, irrespective of who will be mad. The truth will assure my happiness.

Promise to always do what is best for *You* at the time, even if others disagree.

It is so hard to buck the system. The system, of course, is society's "We don't see the magnitude of what's going on" attitude as well as our family's, "Don't talk about it, so it didn't happen" attitude. As human beings who want to be accepted and loved by family and friends, the pressure to fall in line with family and societal requests and expectations is great. The pressure is so great that many survivors succumb to it by staying within their shell because the thought of being ostracized by family is more than they can bear. When survivors make this choice, it's almost as if they have chosen what they believe to be the best option. In reality, it's the worst option. Yes, being ostracized by family and certain elements of your community is terrible, but isn't dying inside worse? Isn't living your life with a two-ton refrigerator on your chest from the pressure to keep the secret in worse? Isn't not being able to fully give of yourself to yourself or anyone else worse? Isn't it worse to live your life filled to the brim with emotions and confusion and distrust? Isn't being unable to fulfill your dreams and aspirations horrible? Why would you not want to be your authentic self? Last I read, women, on average, live until their mid-80's. Is this how you want to live for your remaining years? Of course not! So what do you need to do? Remember The Acceptance "Accept the fact that your family, partner, or closest friend may never respond or react in quite the way you need them to or when you need them to. You may have to construct a new family."

I Promise to always do what is best for me at the time, even if others disagree.

Give yourself permission to take care of your physical & mental health. Love your body! Develop your mind!

A common theme I have noticed amongst most incest and child sexual survivors is confusion and sometimes panic about our bodies. It's as if the initial violation of our bodies is not enough because we can be left with a lifetime of disdain for our beautiful bodies. It seems we can be at any period of time either hyper-vigilant about our bodies or totally let ourselves go "to pot."

When I am referring to the hyper-vigilant Sista, I'm referring to the Sista who daily adorns her body with clothes, jewelry, make-up, weekly hair do's, piercing, tattoos, etc. to such an extreme that her adornments are not for her but for the outside world She literally cannot make a quick run to the corner store without adorning herself as if she going to a "dress-up" event. This Sista is tired. Keeping up the outside facade is a lot of work! The Sista who lets herself go is just as tired. She is tired of feeling like she is a sexual object. She lets herself go because she thinks she will be invisible to the outside world.

Considering all of what you have achieved up to this point in your recovery, and considering the Promises and Permissions are your "maintenance plan," you must give your yourself permission to fully love your body and develop your mind. What this means is that when you are adorning your body, you are now doing it because YOU feel good inside and out. It means you no longer have the need to feel invisible because you know YOU are important and what you have to contribute to the world is of value and importance.

Giving yourself Permission to love your body also means you are okay with being twenty pounds overweight or underweight. You're okay with your too curly or too straight hair. You're okay with being 30, 45, 68 years of age. You're okay with your disabilities or impairments. It means you love your pale or ebony skin, slightly crooked nose, or voluptuous hips.

Giving yourself permission to take care of your physical & mental health, loving your body and developing your mind also means you are okay being the oldest person in a college classroom or a GED class. Go ahead and snicker at being glad you have already gone through what your junior classmates have yet to experience as they mature. Giving yourself Permission to develop your mind also means you have started reading books and magazines for pleasure; maybe you're volunteering for a non-profit, or you have started working formally or informally with other survivors. You're taking care of yourself!

I give myself Permission to take care of my physical & mental health. Love my body! Develop my mind!

Promise to give yourself Permission to forgive yourself of ANYTING and EVERYTING you have done to survive. Your higher power forgave you long time ago.

You may notice that this Promise and Permission is also an Acceptance. I felt it necessary that this topic be addressed in both areas because it seems to be one of the toughest areas for many survivors to reconcile with. It's tough because of what some survivors have done to get through their darkest moments. This is not an area that once you accept the deeds you have done in the past to survive, that you will not be triggered in this area again because you probably will. Oftentimes this trigger is brought into our lives by people who refuse to allow us to be the happy person we are today, but instead want to keep us in our past. Who knows why some toxic people have problems with others improving their life. Call them "haters" or maybe they are just plain old jealous. Who knows; who cares? Your focus has to be on the belief that your higher power has forgiven you and hopefully most, if not all, the important people in your life have forgiven you as well. Your focus must be maintained on the belief that at this point in your recovery, your goal is to use your past to continue sculpturing your bright future and to help other survivors who may still be in the dark part of their journey to happiness.

I Promise to give myself Permission to forgive myself of ANYTHING and EVERYTHING I have done to survive. My higher power forgave me long time ago.

The PROMISES AND PERMISSIONS

I.   I Promise to remember my triggers and immediately invoke my "trigger buster" strategies when triggered.

II. I give myself Permission to be really, really, really mad, angry, and/or enraged about being sexually abused and how it has affected my life.

III. I Promise to openly share my story to keep sexual abuse of children in everyone's face.

IV. I give myself Permission to tell the truth, irrespective of who will be mad. The truth will assure my happiness.

V.   I Promise to always do what is best for me at the time, even if others disagree.

VI. I give myself Permission to take care of my physical & mental health. Love my body! Develop my mind!

VII. I Promise to give myself Permission to forgive myself of ANYTHING and EVERYTHING I have done to survive. My higher power forgave me long time ago.

BIBLIOGRAPHY

AND

RESOURCES

Multiple Ways To Develop Your Mind

Bibliography

Bass, Ellen, and Davis, Laura. *The Courage To Heal: A guide for Women Survivors of Child Sexual Abuse.* Harper Perennial, New York, 1994

Bass, Ellen, et. al. *Free Your Mind. The Book for Gay, Lesbian, and Bisexual Youth and their Allies.* Harper Perennial, New York, 1996

Blume, Sue. *Secret Survivors: Uncovering Incest and its After Effects in Women.* Balantine Books, New York 1990

Broach-Sowles, Holly. *Childhood Sexual Abuse 101: Not an Elective.* Khori Publishers, Cincinnati, Ohio 1998

Coleman, Eli, et. al. *Sex Offender Treatment: Biological Dysfunction, Intrapsychic Conflict, Interpersonal Violence.* Haworth Press, Inc., New York, 1996

Engel, Beverly. *The Right to Innocence: Healing the Trauma of Childhood Sexual Abuse.* St. Martin's Press, New York 1989

Gil, Eliana, et. al. *Sexualized Children: Assessment and Treatment of Sexualized Children and Children Who Molest.* Dell Publishing, New York, NY 1983

Jenkins, Phillip, *Pedophiles and Priests: Anatomy Of A Contemporary Crisis.* Oxford University Press, Oxford, NY 1996

Johnson, Cavanagh, Toni. *Understanding Your Child's Sexual Behavior. What's Natural and Healthy? New Harbinger Publisher*

Lew, Mike. *Victims No Longer: Men Recovering From Incest and Other Sexual Child Abuse.* HarperCollins, New York, 1986

Rafanello, Donna. *Can't Touch My Soul: A Guide for Lesbian Survivors of Child Sexual Abuse.* Alyson Publications, 2004

Robinson, Lori. *I Will Survive.* Seal Press, New York, New York, 2002

Russell, Diana. *The Secret Trauma: Incest in the Lives of Girls and Women.* Basic Books, New York, NY, 1986,1999

Salter, Ana, Ph.D. *Predators, Pedophiles, Rapists, and Other Sex Offenders who they are, how they operate, and how we can protect ourselves and our children.* Basic Books, New York, NY, 2003

Stone, Robin. *No Secrets No Lies. How Black Families Can Heal from Sexual Abuse.* Broadway Books, New York 2004

Resources

Nirvanan Now!
P.O. Box 2444
Toledo, OH 43606
(419) 729-0245
www.mynirvananow.org

An organization whose vision is that every child will grow up in a safe, loving environment and sexual abuse survivors will be provided support and assistance during their recovery. Organization offers educational trainings, life coaching services, survivor support groups, and maintains a speakers bureau. Founder, CeCe Norwood, MA

National Children's Alliance
1612 K Street NW, Suite 500
Washington DC 20006
(800) 239-9950
www.nca-online.org

A nonprofit organization that helps communities establish and improve children's advocacy centers which serve abused children and their families.

Advocates for Abused and Battered Lesbians (AABL)
www.aablorg

Girls Fight Back
www.girlsfightback.com

Inspires, motivates, and educates women and girls to take a proactive stance opposing and combating violence against women.

Darkness to Light
247 Meeting Street
Charleston, SC
(834) 965-5444
www.darkness2light.org

A nonprofit organization that seeks to reduce child sexual abuse nationally through education and public awareness aimed at adults.

The National Children's Advocacy Center
210 Pratt Avenue
Huntsville, AL 35801
(256) 533-5437
www.nationalcac.org

A nonprofit agency providing prevention, intervention, and treatment services to physically and sexually abused children.

Rape, Abuse & Incest National Network (RAINN)
635 Pennsylvania Avenue SE
Washington, DC 20003
(800) 656-4673
www.rainn.org

One of the nation's largest anti-sexual assault organization which has programs to prevent sexual assault, help victims, and ensure rapists are brought to justice. 24-hr crisis and referral online and by phone.

Healing Journey Survivor chat room
www.healing-journey.net/chat.html

Incest Survivors Anonymous
P.O. Box 17245
Long Beach CA 90807-7245
(562) 428-5599

Kristen's Place
www.nhhi.net/kp

Provides tools for lesbian and straight survivors of sexual abuse/assault, recovery, support forum, chat, on-line counseling

Survivors of Incest Anonymous
World Service Office, P.O. Box 190
Benson, MD 21018-9998
(410) 893-3322
www.siawso.org

Organization that services adult men and women who were sexually abused as children.

The Safer Society Foundation, Inc.
P.O. Box 340
Brandon VT 05733
(802) 247-3132
www.safersociety.org

A nonprofit national research advocacy and referral center. Offers a variety of books, cassettes, and videos for offenders, victims, family, and professionals.

Black Women's Health Imperative (formerly the National Black Women's Health Project)
600 Pennsylvania Avenue SE, Suite 310
Washington Dc 20003
(202) 548-4000
www.blackwomenshealth.org

A leading education, research, advocacy, and leadership development institution for Black women's health concerns.

Rosa Parks Sexual Assault Crisis Center
4182 S. Western Avenue
Los Angeles, CA 90062
(223) 290-4119

Provides support and counseling for children and adults.

National Resource Center on Child Sexual Abuse
106 Lincoln Street
Huntsville, AL 35801
(800) KIDS-006

V day
www.vday.org

Promotes events to increase awareness, raise money and revitalize the spirit of existing antiviolence organizations to stop sexual and domestic violence against women and girls.

Pandora's Box
www.prevent-abuse-now.com/index.htm

Forum for child abuse information, including child protection resources, research and statistics on child sexual abuse, prevention resources, legal information, and poetry.

Justice for Children
733 15th Street NW, Suite 214
Washington DC 20005
(202) 462-4688 www.jfcadvocacy.org

An organization that advocates for children's protection from abuse. Maintains a lawyer referral list by state.

Association of Black Psychologists
P.O. Box 5999
Washington DC 20040-5999
(202) 722-0808
www.abpsi.org

Provides a national listing of Black psychologist

Prevent Child Abuse America
200 S. Michigan Avenue Suite 17
Chicago, IL 60604
(312) 663-3520
www.preventchildabuse.org

Survivors Healing Center
2301 Mission St., Suite C-1
Santa Cruz CA 95060
(831) 423-7601

Provides resources, classes, and healing support for survivors of childhood sexual abuse

Voices in Action, Inc. (Victims of Incest Can Emerge Survivors)
8041 Hosbrook, Suite 236
Cincinnati OH 45236
(800) 786-4238 www.voices-action.org

International network of male and female incest survivors, local groups, that offer free referrals to therapist, agencies, and self-help group endorsed by survivors

National Sexual Violence Resource Center
123 N. Enola Drive
Enola PA 17025
www.nsvrc.org
(877) 739-3895

Works with researchers to provide advocates with current information on various topics related to sexual violence.

Survivors Network of those Abuse by Priest (SNAP)
www.teleport.com/snapmail/

Self help organization of men and women who were sexually abused by priests, brothers, nuns, deacons, teachers, etc.

Crimes Against Children Research Center
University of New Hampshire
20 College Road
Durham NH 03824
(603) 862-1888
www.unhedu/ccrc

Center focus is the victimization of children and adolescents inside and outside of the family.

Child Molestation Research and Prevention Institute
110 Piedmont Avenue
Atlanta GA 30309
(404) 872-5152
Oakland CA 94602
(510) 530-7980
www.stopchildmolestation.org

Organization that promotes education, research, and family support.

Male Survivor: The National Organization Against Male Sexual Victimization
PMB 103,5505
Connecticut Avenue NW
Washington DC 20015
(800) 738-4181
www. malesuvivor. org

National organization dedicated to preventing, healing, and eliminating sexual victimization of boys and men through treatment, research, education, advocacy, and activism.